Conditions
and
Cures

Conditions
and
Cures

Ken Waldman

STEEL TOE BOOKS
BOWLING GREEN, KENTUCKY

ISBN 0-9743264-4-5

Cover Design by Kathy McInnis
Book Design by Joelean Copeland

Steel Toe Books
Department of English
135 Cherry Hall
Western Kentucky University
1 Big Red Way
Bowling Green, KY 42101-3576

Grateful acknowledgment is made to the editors of the
following journals in which some of these poems, or
versions of these poems, first appeared:

Arts and Letters "W.C. Fields Meets Abbott and Costello"
Border Voices 11 "A Happier Doctor"
Convolvulus "The Rewind"
First Circle "Kvetching in Malay"
Flyway "Dyxlesia;" "Stutterer;" "To End the Slaughter;" "Wart
    Stories"
The Gamut "Three Lessons in Taking Off Clothes"
Many Mountains Moving "The Best Dancers That Night"
Mobius "My Father, Ralph Kramden"
Natural Bridge "Buster Keaton, Romancer;" "Charlie Chaplin
    Goes to Heaven; " "Woody Allen Addresses a New Age
    Convention"
New Mexico Humanities Review "She Was Tired of Men"
Plainsongs "Rodney Dangerfield Finds Respect"
Puerto del Sol "Screenplay"
Sundog, The Southeast Review "Double Mastectomy"
West Branch "Aunt Joyce Recalls Meeting Uncle Max;"
    "Growling Old Woman, Grumbling Old Man"
Yalobusha Review "Depressed Thumb"

Contents

I

II

III

IV

I

The Condition

The malady defies diagnosis,
thrums anxiety, refers
to a host of disorders—
bad skin, migraine, chest pain,
depression, fatigue, insomnia,
infections, an assortment
of -ologies and -itises
and manias—and short,
hot, ecstatic, strange,
passionate flights that fire
like rockets, disappearing
as grit in long slow blue.
This is our orbit, friend.
To live it is the cure.

Kvetching in Malay

I have to admit I'm feeling odd
about my health. No matter
what I do, God's
a pain in the bladder.

About my health, no matter.
A pain in the neck, the ass,
a pain in the bladder.
You'd think God would pass

a pain in the neck, the ass
to someone more in need.
You'd think God would pass
my sharp pains, indeed,

to someone more in need,
like a thieving somebody.
My sharp pains. Indeed,
my bladder. Like moldy putty.

Like a thieving somebody.
What did I do, God?
My bladder, like moldy putty.
I have to admit I'm feeling odd.

Good Eater

His ample ass didn't just sit
on the diner counter stool,
but swallowed it, this uncorked man
who gracelessly plopped—
big flanks brushing
irked patrons on either side—
to consume six fried eggs, sausage,
hash browns, toast, oatmeal,
two donuts, a quart of coffee.

Don't tell him to diet.
Content to waddle and wheeze,
this four-hundred-pounder's bound
to mom, who plied his childhood
with seconds and thirds of potatoes,
gravy, sweets, and then promised
sunny days if he ate. A dutiful boy.

Double Mastectomy

Soon after the death
of her second husband,
my grandma Joyce
had both breasts cut.
Cancer. She came
to live with us.
I was fifteen, cute,
but a prude.

One morning I cracked
the bathroom door.
Grandma stood before
a mirror, posing
in her panties.
Modeling, she looked
like a skinny boy
who had shriveled.

That night I called Clay,
a guy in my class
I knew liked me.
We went to a movie.
In the theater, taking
his hand, I had him
touch me there,
there, then there.

New Angels

A cute teenage couple
cruising the local Safeway
bought enough honey,
whipped cream, syrup,
coconut oil to make
the cashier guffaw.

No crude joke, the pair
of juniors in love
with lust were hungry
to open bright wings, flap,
and snatch that sticky-
sweet ache of God.

Three Lessons in Taking Off Clothes

Enthusiasts choose exclamation points—
Undress! Disrobe! Shed!—
denying that wool, cotton, silk cost
money. No sense ripping
good fabric on sharp barbs.
The first lesson:
If you care about clothes,
use your hands.

The actual procedure varies.
Some begin by unbuckling
belts. Others unbutton shirts,
untie shoes, unzip pants, slip
out of skirts. All methods work
as long as progress is steady.
The second lesson: Invite a friend
to take your clothes off for you.

The third lesson: Dive naked
into the sheets. Pull your partner
toward you. Rub knuckles.
Run fingertips. Grab anything
that moves. Wrestle and tickle.
Fumble. Grip and squeeze.
Hold tight until taut.
Let go with a shout.

Screenplay

Honeydew Butterfish, maybe smartest girl
ever from Asheboro, North Carolina,
winner of piano scholarship to Harvard.

Willie Silver, aspiring writer and comic,
Harvard Lampoon assistant editor,
former metropolitan St. Louis spelling bee champ.

The Lampoon Halloween party. Honeydew,
mimicking Billie Holiday, lullabies
Willie, wisecracking behind a Woody Allen mask.

Willie falls. Honeydew catches, invites
Willie to Asheboro for Christmas, gets invited
to St. Louis for New Year's. Neither home

opens. Back in Cambridge, Willie and Dew
fight while walking along the Charles.
If you don't move in with me, Honeydew,

Willie declares, I'll find someone new.
You're not telling this black girl what to do,
Honeydew answers, turning away. For a month

the lovers suffer glimpses of one another
in classroom building hallways, in delicatessen
windows, in passing subway cars. For Valentine's,

Willie sends a sunflower, a rose, and a note
to meet him Sunday noon at the Commons' pond.
Honeydew arrives to find Willie showing off

two pairs of skates. Lacing hers, Honeydew says
you crazy man I've never been on ice in my life.
Me either, says Willie, ankles wobbling as he tries

to glide, hilariously plops. They elope in March,
perfect sunshine, but first a last shot of the lovers
leaving the courthouse, necking, naming dreams—

she to be Thelonious Monk's daughter, he
Mark Twain's true heir. And so they've named it:
their fleshy fumbling coupling, the music of ink.

Aunt Joyce Recalls Meeting Uncle Max

I must've thought him a ghost,
so skedaddled to the ladies lounge
where I sat bug-eyed a spell
beside the broken lamp and my pal
Lucille who smoked Luckies
and was so beautifully mad,
her hair a wild platinum swirl.
When she asked me about him,
I said how his lips were like a lock,
his crooked teeth like traps,
how he liked cracking his knuckles,
and wore an orange-brown shirt
I thought mixed fire with dirt.
What long legs he had, I told her.
And how I loved them, loved *him*,
though, of course, I didn't know him
at all. So marry him, Lucille said,
her green eyes so crazy fabulous,
her laugh a silvery cackling.

How that night turned and turned,
and turned into infinity.

The Marriage Thing

for Pratap and Sue

Marriage? A foreign thing,
necessarily, between man and woman.
A good thing, I'm thinking.

A thing that inevitably is lacking
sense, but still sucks people in.
Marriage, a foreign thing,

some say, laughing or winking,
loving the folly. Wife? Husband?
A good thing, I'm thinking,

if you know what you're getting
into. A difficult thing. A challenge.
Marriage is a foreign thing,

I'm thinking, weighing this, weighing
that, weighing the word *foreign*.
A good thing, I'm thinking,

foreign, for we're always crossing
borders, acting the alien again and again.
Marriage? A foreign thing?
A good thing? I'm thinking.

Growling Old Woman, Grumbling Old Man

I've run out of patience, old man.
You've given me an ulcer this holiday,
you, the big wheel, spending Christmas Eve
in a tavern buying drinks for the house—
you call that normal? What's normal?
I've seen you look at our darling
granddaughter like you're some lovesick soldier
wounded in the chest. Old man,
I invite you to respond. Go on,
tell me to quit blubbering. God knows,
I never said I was perfect—
look, I've worn your lousy gold ring
for thirty-five years, worn it
like a trap. I'm not one to judge,
believe me, but you don't know the axe handle
from the axe. I hate going on like this.
And watch the cream in my coffee.
You know I like it black.

I know how you like your coffee—
drinking so much gave you the ulcer,
made you miserable and bitchy.
And I know how you're not perfect—
I've spent almost forty years
staying out of your imperfect way.
And I know how you worry for our granddaughter—
it's keeping with your usual behavior;
by the way, I've never touched her.
And I know how you hated this Christmas Eve—
you didn't add, did you, how you hated
last Christmas Eve, when I stayed home.
And I know how you'll twist these words—

you'd love to be my death, wouldn't you,
but I plan on living forever.
Old woman, I know you like I know myself.
Now hurry up and drink your coffee.
We needed to leave an hour ago.

Ronald and Vivian

Viv, for the last time
I'm asking you to please sit down
on this hickory swing
so we can swing gently
and hold hands like we did
our first date. Remember
that night? My great history-
making smooch? The big wet one?
And your tongue sliding in
like a snake. Viv, that first kiss
took all my nerve—no wonder
I fell. Viv, what's wrong?
You can't be tired of me
after all we've shared.
Vivian, don't you see? Vivian?
I've apologized a thousand times
for being too pushy. I promise
to change—we'll do it your way.
Just stop acting like this—
the silent treatment drives me crazy.

Scrabble

The man and woman were playing
for blood.
        "Prize," he said,
sticking the *z* on the pink star
in the middle of the board.
"32 points."
        "Zoea," she said,
smirking, getting rid of three
of her seven vowels.
        "Infuse,"
he said, making *zoeas*.
        "Enigma,"
she said, pointing at him,
complaining as she placed the tiles.

"Parched," he said, "for fourteen
times two. Double word score."

"Fuck you," she said, seeing *doughy*
on her rack, and wondering
where oh where her seventh,
the i, had disappeared.

She Was Tired of Men

The Christmas after her 40th birthday she asked
    that her first-born son, the accident, hang from a
    monkey bar;
that her younger boy, the mistake, suffocate in a
    paper bag;
that her ex, the louse, fall asleep smoking and torch
    his condo;
that her brother, Mr. Know-it-all, open a mail bomb;
that her lawyer, the smooth-talking loudmouth,
    guzzle a gallon of Gatorade laced with rat poison;
that her internist, the flirt, wither from AIDS;
that her boss, the bastard, suffer a coronary and
    drown in an Acupulco bathtub;
that her banker, the cheapskate idiot coward, blow
    his brains out at Russian roulette;
that her first true love, the liar, slide off a roof and
    crack his head open on asphalt;
that her current beau, the nobody, vanish;
that her father, long dead, toss and turn and moan
    forever;
that God, the chauvinist, choke on a forkful of pork
    chop;
that Santa Claus, the jolly slob, drive his sleigh head-
    on into an avalanche.

Nadine Can't Sleep

Counting iguana,
crocodile, sheep,
Nadine can't sleep.
Maybe tomorrow.

A couple of days
turn into weeks.
Nadine can't sleep.
Maybe a lay?

What did she miss?
She brings home Rip.
Nadine can't sleep.
Rip does, then leaves pissed.

Next night, awake,
and feeling cheap,
Nadine can't sleep.
And the headache,

like an abyss
decades deep.
Nadine can't sleep,
convinced

she'll die of fatigue,
a migrained heap.
Nadine can't sleep,
though is intrigued:

this pain like a light's
flash, an answering machine's beep.
Nadine can't sleep,
decides to write

what she swore
and swore she'd keep.
Nadine can't sleep.
It's as bad as before,

this scribbling the truth
about the rapes.
Nadine can't sleep.
Horrible truths:

each word a clue,
each line a leap.
Nadine can't sleep
until she's through

reliving the nights
that seeped.
Nadine can't sleep.
Horror. Fright.

Pages of truth.
Dad said: *Not a peep.*
Nadine can't sleep.
Her youth

ravaged by her father.
His breath. Feet.
Nadine can't sleep.
Her creepy father.

She was five or six.
One night she couldn't sleep.
Nadine can't sleep.
So his father sticks

his thing in.
Nadine can't sleep.
Nadine can't sleep.
He does it again

and again, Nadine,
Nadine, go to sleep.
Nadine can't sleep,
a machine,

a piston pumping,
Nadine feeling spilled heat,
Nadine can't sleep,
feels like jumping

out the window,
Nadine can't sleep,
Nadine can't sleep,
until she's out the window,

until she leaps,
until she leaps,
Nadine can't sleep
until she leaps

into the night.
Until she leaps.
Nadine can't sleep.
Until she flies.

To Jim, Who Fell Off a Roof

When told how your twelve foot drop
tore diaphragm and stomach,
almost broke your back, I thought,
wait, this couldn't have been

an accidental fall, bad luck
stalking some innocent man—
this was your test to receive
new wings. Friend, good news—

you passed. The next pair
of flaps are on order,
the best: silvery feathers,
extra-long span, a proper fit

for balance, safety, strength.
So relax. Rest sore shoulders.
Imagine lovely take-off and flight.
You'll be up gliding soon.

Weathermaker

Suppose your life is lost
in an office or marriage,
days passing like Alaska
winter months, your dreams—
the few you sense—
a dark catalogue
you're scared to recall.

Suppose you've wasted
this last long decade
unconsciously becoming
what you hate, a whiner
who pouts about blown
fortune, frozen fate,
ice fog and horizontal sleet.

Suppose you say *enough*.
Fly into the light
of a newborn self, letting
slip your dead weight
skin. Then rise above
that final cold slope
of mountain within.

The Attorney

For weeks her best sleep
has been tested by the thumping
of Mr. Flopsy, the pet rabbit
that's taken the dark space
beneath the bed and filled it
with his slow frantic rhythm,
sporadic raps on hardwood
like knocking from inside

a coffin. No sense silencing
a hare that taps the code
of her own panicky heart.
Still single, defined by work,
the insistent beating below
marks the ungodly hour
between anxiety and faith,
the recognition of death.

//

To End the Slaughter

Imagine these clean
black typeset letters
in the original,
traced by fountain pen,
the cartridge ink
a smeary red gush
of blood. Alas,
this neat page
you now hold
is one more proof
most pain—
like a 3 a.m. panic
that jumps from the gut—
can't be translated.
To quit butchering
your life, remake
the messy core
of your messy self,
step by messy step.
In the bowels—
the primal healing:
tell your story.

Cardiology

Two doctors disagree—an attack or not—
in the study of a muscle that has pumped
without complaint for almost fifty years,

but for a brief flare of pressure—several seconds
of attention-getting—nine days before.
Afterwards, tightness, some tenderness, strain.

The morning it happened, I'd been paying bills,
anxious about debt. The previous afternoon
I'd ridden my bike, felt the heart thump hard

as I pedaled fifty yards straight uphill.
Easier now to gather my own verdict,
to ask the heart what it wants and needs,

to offer it a stage. How I'd love to hear
everything is fine, that I can quit my worry.
But all I get is a slow steady beat,

the same stoic pace. Putting an ear closer,
I imagine the whisper: *I know you're lonely*
single, afraid to die. And how you're strong,

which makes it so difficult to let go
and change. Lucky you, to realize this chance.
It's not too late, friend. It's not too late.

More difficult now to re-enter that old world
where a heart neither whispers nor talks,
remains mostly mute to the pleasures and the hurts.

Chest Episode

for Gary Balfantz

It was just a little squeeze,
a short hug, something
tugging like a nearing deadline.

Heart attack.
            The phrase appeared
abstractly, dispassionately, as in oh,
I better watch out—or else.
                    The next week
I allowed myself fatigue, treated myself
gingerly, ate smartly, noted each transient
ache or pain. Married to myself,
I needed to take better care.
How was I to find, and keep,
the lovely woman I so desired
if I couldn't even honor
my own precious body.
                    For once,
I had no urge to rush,
and when I did find myself
rifling through files to find photos,
reviews, and clips—my typical work—
I felt awful and tense, like Mother's Day
twenty years earlier when mid-shift,
just like that, I decided
I no longer had what it took
to wait tables on busy nights.
                    For reassurance,
I visited a clinic—blood pressure: normal;
EKG: low—and was prescribed a card
with the name of a cardiologist.
That night I slept poorly, woke
before 5. Saturday, friends in town

suggested the local university hospital,
the ER if necessary. My one open day,
a full week ahead, freely enjoying
the cool crisp March air, I didn't think twice
that I'd just ambled two miles
in the direction of the big medical center,
sidetracked twice because of fenced
construction zones, witnessed
a minor car crash, all in order to sign myself
into an emergency room.
                              Within five minutes
I was met by a nurse, two med techs,
a doctor, an attending doctor. In turn,
I was wired, probed, pricked, needled,
then wheeled for chest x-rays.
Blood pressure: normal. EKG: reasonable.
The gestalt of this, the first doc said,
referring, I understood, to lifestyle,
travel, perhaps even politics
and art, *is that you should be admitted
overnight, likely for a few days.*
The EKG, now within range,
was explained to mean nothing
in itself: like any process, it needed
to be examined over time.
                              Quickly
I calculated how I might have
spent maybe a grand the past hour,
and now was looking at another.
This week I had almost three grand
in job contracts. Factoring in
credit card debt, the utter lack
of insurance, I shook my head:
even if I wanted, I couldn't afford
hospitalization at this point; I'd only

come to be checked. *But you're risking*
your life, the boss doctor added,
and you can't look at risk like this.
We need to be sure.   I was left alone
a half hour to mull the choice
before my primary doc reappeared
to explain the surprise of an enzyme level
in the blood, and how, probably,
the week before I'd suffered a heart attack.

Heart attack?
                    No, no, certainly not,
I'd have said if I were normal,
but what could be normal here, wires all over,
hooked to an IV, my thumb pinched
between plastic clasps, a machine charting
thin gold, green, blue lines, zigzags
and arcs, a mechanical art.
Instead of arguing, I felt myself slip
as I listened to this doc say
I'd be admitted as soon as possible
to the seventh floor, be kept a few days,
maybe longer, undergo more tests,
then most likely a procedure
where they'd stick a catheter
up my groin into my heart
to assess damage
and clear the block. They left me
alone then to the panic
of a complicated and beautiful life
suddenly stunted. So many phone calls:
the cancellations, the reordering
of everything. I saw my credit card debt
of twenty-five grand climbing
just like that to thirty,

then thirty-five as I'd sit
the next weeks cursing my ailing heart,
the stupidity, and wondering
what next. A woman entered
with a phone so I could make
a single call. She had a form to sign,
something about a will. Punching
the number of my local friends—
a busy signal. Explaining my fears—
and the complexity of my affairs—
I began crying, and the woman left
to summon a social worker,
who seemed unable to comprehend
the despair. No assets,
a million undone tasks, and now
I'm told I've suffered a heart attack—
I'm scared to death, I said.

      The internist
on duty happened by then, asked questions,
so I retold the story, quivering. Highly unlikely
you've suffered an attack, he said,
explaining the enzyme level, the lone
indicator of life-altering dysfunction,
was still 99% normal. He left,
recommending I admit myself
overnight for observation—
offering I might even be discharged
in time to work Monday.

      And then I lay
alone the next forty minutes,
breathing in, breathing out, empty
of most everything, save the occasional
whimpers of someone in difficulty,
the curtained space beside mine.
When the first doc checked back,
I mentioned what the internist said.

We disagree completely on this—
I don't know what he's thinking;
normal is 0 and you have a reading—
your levels last week would likely
have been higher. This is no joke.
You need to be admitted.
                    I returned
to my breath, slowly in, slowly out,
and studied the curtain, the walls,
my pants draped over a chair
three feet away, my sweater bundled
in the seat, my shoes and socks
on the floor beneath. I let myself go,
even longer, slower, steadier breaths,
let go the old man nearby in distress,
let go the past days, weeks, months,
and the years slid by next, all history
a blur, and from some depth noted
a murmur—*it's a mistake to be admitted—*
though couldn't say if I'd said it
or heard it, from inside or out.
The next minute an attendant arrived
to wheel me upstairs: the room
was ready. *Wait,* I said, *let me talk*
to the doc—I think I'm going to bail.

Heart attack, we think you had
a heart attack, said the doctor
who first diagnosed me. *Sure,*
you can walk outside,
but no guarantee a cardiologist
will have time here free this month;
you're at risk.

                    Seeing me shake
my head no, he sighed:
If you leave, you'll have to sign
a form that you're doing this
without our consent, a chance
you might die, or suffer
brain damage. If you do go,
make an appointment somewhere
this week and take two aspirins daily,
at the least.
                              I thanked that doc
and the internist, who stopped by again
to repeat that I should remain,
but should also trust my judgment
and intuition, wherever they might lead.

Once the IV was unhooked,
I signed papers, undid wires, removed tape,
donned socks, shoes, shirt, sweater,
slowly walked down two halls, through a door,
and back out to the vast, imperfect, ongoing world.

Sore Chest

Eighteen days after the short spasm
inside, my chest presses for answers.
Damage, I shudder to say, then shut
my eyes to journey inside. Yes
and no, the problem deeper
than I imagine, and nothing
to do with the muscle. Damage?
Not exactly, and nothing
that can be explained in a language
of medicine. But damage, yes,
if you can name *damage* the surfacing
of this last painful layer, the recognition
of every past failure of the heart,
its losses, its terrors, its history,
this most awful quest for love.

Villanelle for my Heart

for Dr. Dawn McGuire and for Lynda Koolish

I'd been concerned about my heart,
had felt off. This, an unsettled time.
You knew where to start:

the history. We sat a few feet apart
and talked. The room smelled of lemon and lime.
I'd been concerned about my heart,

I said. Several weeks earlier, a cat-clawing dart
of pain. Then, a sense of dirt, failure, slime.
You knew where to start:

you listened, watched, performed your art—
stethoscope to my chest, metal shiny as a dime.
I'd been concerned about my heart,

feared unaffordable loss, the saddest wart,
disability or worse. You didn't have to know why;
you knew where. *To start,*

you said, *lay out your every last part*
on clean cloth in sun. Soak off the grime,
and the concern. About your heart,
you know where to start.

Heartwash

Enter the twilit room and close your eyes
gently, allowing a soft self-indulgent flutter.
Seated now, soon you'll dream you're between
hypnosis and sleep. The technician,
a scrubbed ghost, will slide through skin,
fascia, ribs, and shrink inside, slipping

like a spy within the greasy thick mix.
Fingering a miniature flask, this attendant
appears as if out of sky, clear gloves so tight
you can almost hear the crackle. A sprinkling
of several drops. A shake. Then a misty spray
from out of the nozzle. The wetness settles.

Later, pale alien receding, a last spot
of liquid evaporating, asked to say what
happened, you'll awaken and touch your chest.
No visible sign of the previous night's
encounter. The only scar a fresh red line
in the psyche, a continuing uncertainty.

The State of My Heart

Six months since I sat, pen in hand,
checkbook open, poised to pay
the latest round of bills. Happy to be extra-
prompt, set to stuff envelopes, seal them,
stick on the stamps, thinking *that* problem
solved for the month, I felt dull pain.
And that quickly, my interior quake, a 2.1,
something that registered, sure, but mild,
no damage, though a warning of a pile
shifting, my body tiring. A half-year later,
still broke and alone, I'm eating better,
feeling fitter. I dream another twenty-five,
thirty years, or more, still strive
for a wife: now a beautiful partner
to share laughs, and a health plan.

Medicine Cabinet

Go ahead. Rummage through
my homeopathic remedies:
the syphilis extract (for the dregs
of an auto-immune disease),
the gold extract (for anger
stuffed through this lifetime),
the snake venom extract
(for I forget what—heart?
joint pains?? memory???).
Read the label on the gels
for pesky athlete's foot.
Shake the hydrogen peroxide
if you want. Compare
my brand of toothpaste
and dental floss to yours.
Chew a vitamin. Study
a few more of my poems.

///

Comedy Hour

I was greatly elated by the discovery that there is a
physiological basis for the ancient theory that laughter is
good medicine—Norman Cousins

Hardy Beseeches Laurel to Hurry

Now look what you've done. How can you stand there,
a silly grin on your face, when we're late
for our audition. This is a big date—
surely you didn't forget, wouldn't *dare*
forget, would you? Come *on*, Stanley. Your hair's
fine. Put your hat on. And yes, you look great.
What, Stan. No, the audition is not at eight.
Seven, Stanley. Seven. We've got to be there
in one half hour, and it's on the far end
of town. Did you hear me? Stan, we must hurry.
Why are you so very slow? I can't depend
on you for anything. Stan, we must hurry.
What, Stan. *Now* you want to practice our act?
Oh, all right. Climb on. You can go piggy-back.

***

Buster Keaton, Romancer

Half stoneface, half sourpuss, the dour
young suitor, dismissed by his beloved,
tumbles from the porch, a miffed glance above
as he takes his pratfall in the flowers,
his dark eyes part rage, part pout, part glower,
a huffy scowl slowly easing as he's moved
to sniff the garden's roses. By *Jove*
rolls on-screen to signify the whiff. Our
hero lifts himself from the dirt, brushes
clung soil off his trousers, stoops to pick
a few fine long-stemmed petals, then rushes
up the steps. His girl warily accepts, sticks
the bouquet in a vase. Six words appear:
Thus starts the lover's promising career.

43

***

Crosby and Hope: The Road to Hollywood Golf Club

Bing, do you know where we're going—you've been
driving for an hour and we're supposed to
tee off at eleven. Now now, Bob, are you
going to doubt me after all we've seen—
Rio, Bali, Morocco, Singapore. I mean
this is Los Angeles, I'm Bing, your true-blue
buddy of a pal...*Then get us there in two*
short minutes, pal. Bob, just look at the ninth green
to the left, that big windblown flag waving
like some beautiful girl. *Bing, that great girl's*
waving you bye-bye. What are you, a raving
loony—your flag's a small tree with a squirrel
running up it, your green's someone's yard. Say,
Bob, take the wheel—you've got a feel for L.A.

***

W.C. Fields Meets Abbott and Costello

Barkeep, a drink for my two new friends here.
The fellows look dry as my mother-in-law's yard—
prettiest spot in Death Valley. You, pard,
what's your name. Just bought you a nickel beer,
didn't I? You, the quick-thinking blade near
the pickled eggs. Quiet, you rotund wild card,
you sanctimonious flab-barrel of lard,
you slobbering big-reared monkey, a mere
baboon. I'm talking to your sidekick, who—
hiccup—looks like the bossman of this crew.
Mr. Bud Abbott, is it? This, uh, deal
is a once-or-twice-in-a-lifetime steal.
Boys, I'm selling my dear wife's full-length mink—
her in it. Barkeep—hiccup—three more drinks.

***

Jack Benny Throws a Bash

Hmmm, how to improve on last year's potluck?
This time I better not forget to call
Burns and tell him instead of food, bring all
the silverware and plates—I hate to get stuck
doing dishes. I'll ask Hope to bring duck,
Berle a ham, Rochester a rather tall
lady for Hope, Dennis a very small
writer for Berle. Fred Allen has the bucks
to pay the caterer for the chocolate cake
I ordered. Mary, bless her heart, will make
pigs-in-a-blanket, an old barnyard specialty
I adore. As the genial host, I'll see
to guests, play fiddle, wear a happy face.
Why not? I'm a prince to supply the space.

***

The Three Stooges Cheat Death

Moe: What's with you numbskulls, parking the car
on top of train tracks. Why, I oughta poke
the two of you in the eyes. *Larry:* I broke
the gas gauge. See? *Moe:* Get outa the car
and fill the tank before I stub this cigar
in your face. What, you think I made a joke?
Get going! Scram! *Curly:* Moe, I just woke
from a dream—a big choo-choo came from far
away and… *Larry:* Yikes, he's right! A train's
aiming right for us! Oh god! Curly, Moe—
what'll we do? *Moe:* Peaheads, use your brains.
Move the car. *Curly:* Oh-oh, hold your nose.
I just cut one. *Larry:* We're saved! What luck!
Gas! *Moe:* Step on it. *Curly:* Nyuk, nyuk, nyuk.

***

Groucho Marx, Diplomate of Internal Medicine

Nurse, give the nervous rectum on fifth floor
10 cc's, any tranquilizer we've got.
Wait, nurse, I'll administer the shot
to her behind myself. And nurse, the poor
stomach down the hall needs attention. Or
is it a colon? Never mind. The clot
of sludge is somewhere. Which reminds me not
to forget that insufferable bore
of a pancreas. The clod hasn't paid
for surgery. I should've fixed the spleen
and gall bladder too. And nurse, call an aide.
A liver needs me downstairs, room sixteen.
Prepare mojos, placebos, the penknife.
Pronto, nurse, to save that chimpanzee's life.

***

Charlie Chaplin Goes to Heaven

The sidestep past cops, the chase up a ramp,
the sly duck, the quick jump to a ladder,
the rung-by-rung scramble, the cops madder
and madder, the get-away by the scamp
into the fog, the reappearance by the scamp
before the sun, the mustachioed face gladder
and gladder, the eyes inexplicably sadder,
the light above like a trillion watt lamp,
and still the ladder, the ladder, hands and feet
up the ladder, the wry wink, the scamp's hat
almost blown off by wind, the smile so proud
as the scamp leaps like a cat onto a cloud,
and finds a jew's harp and vaudeville fiddle—
God's fey organ grinder in the middle.

46

Will Rogers' Ghost Shows Up in Nome

Quite a town, Nome. Its fine daily paper,
The Nugget, published every day but six,
comes out on Thursday, I believe. This week
I've read and reread page ten, a caper
involving a young priest, my old neighbor
in fact, who got sick of having to fix
God's ways, as happens, so one night, for kicks,
goes to the Anchor Bar, lets Jim Reaper
buy shot after shot of gin. Man oh man.
The priest maybe thought Jim would just talk.
Or maybe thought when in Nome do as the Nomans.
Found frozen and drunk, the priest maybe thought
he'd live forever, here at the world's end.
But ol' Jim Reaper got to him, my friends.

***

Lenny Bruce Before God

I'll tell you something, lousy cocksucker,
you got nothing on me. You're the sick one
for the spotlight. A filthy ham. I'd be done,
zero, zilch, if it weren't for your damn muck
of a planet. A list, motherfucker,
of your sins: Spics, Niggers, Jews, booze, guns,
drugs. Ah, drugs. Drum roll, please, for the high son
of a bitch who gets off like a hooker
junkie on our pain. You tell us to keep
faith, then turn around and screw us, then turn,
your hand out, take our dough, and fall asleep.
Whore in heaven, dear God, I pray you burn
in hell. But I love you, God. Fuck me, God,
Come on, God. I'm Lenny Bruce. Here's my bod.

My Father, Ralph Kramden

You'd think it was all laughs, having a loud,
coarse, fat comedian of a dad, a dumb
bus driver who treated the world like scum,
belittled his pal, his wife, his son—cowed
us all. He was always right, always proud
of screwing around, always knew "them bums"
downtown wanted him by the balls, the thumbs,
the throat. Our small living room got crowded
as soon as he walked in yelling for his food,
his shirt, his bowling ball, yelling for the sake
of yelling. He never tried to make it work,
my father, prince of the fifties—a no-good
liar and blowhard, the great migraine headache.
My father wasn't funny. He was a jerk.

***

The Mirror Speaks to Jerry Lewis

Look at yourself, a weakling nincompoop
who's made a career playing google-eyed
nitwits, stupendously pesty brain-fried
clowns, frenetic and buck-toothed dupes,
eunuched clods, cracked boneheads, a group
of out-in-out morons all in your tried-
and-true trademark goofiness symbolized
best by dark hair slicked with silly goop.
When I see your obsequious jackass face,
the befuddled look that masks ambition,
I'm embarrassed. You've played the oaf too long,
Jerry, and it's killing you. Have the grace
to change. No, I'm not demanding *Mission
Impossible*. Try outsmarting King Kong.

***

Robin Williams Up Against the Wall

Ah, ugly customer, rough and tough muckface,
take this karate chop to the right brick—
EEEE-yuhhh. Shit, worked with wood. This trick
I learned from my dad—I'm stealing your knee brace,
sport. What? No bum knee? Well, here's a club, ace,
and I'm aiming to tee off on your dick.
No? So I missed. Bet you don't think I'm sick
enough to sneak up, spray some good hot mace
in your eyes, and follow with a quick snatch
of ear. Ha, gotcha. And listen, Van Gogh,
I've scaled lots of you guys, never been scratched.
Tense? Relax, friend. Here's a tablet. Hello,
sucker. You just ate a shrinking pill, scout.
This is your nemesis jumping over and out.

***

Cheech and Chong Off Drugs

You know what's funny, man—I'm just as stoned
straight as I am stoned—I mean it's weird, man,
like I'm high on air. *Air, man?* Yeah, man—
every breath I take it's like reefer just phoned
collect. *Collect, man?* Yeah, man—I'm not stoned,
but I accept that collect call, man, and
I'm flying into orbit—it's like my hands
are wings, man. *Wings, man?* Man, I'm all alone
in space, flapping away like some damn bird,
man, and it's like wow, looking around, seeing
everybody stuck in everyday lives—words
don't say it, man, nothing says it but being
high on air, a bird circling, flapping hands
like wings. *Don't you mean flapping your arms, man?*

Rodney Dangerfield Finds Respect

Look at me. I must be dreaming. What's this—
my darling wifey-pooh's smiling, rubbing my feet,
clipping my toenails. My honey's so sweet,
old beeswax I call her. Hey, no more piss-
and-shit moaning for this guy. Sure I'll miss
the blow-by-blow, the put-downs, the complete
shebang. But now I want to be treated
with respect. Yeah, great big hugs and kisses.
And no more niggling aches and pains—vamoose
bad back. And snookums, how about cooking
a bird tonight, a big one, with enough juice
for a quart of gravy. Ah, we're looking
like angels. I know, toots. This is heaven.
See my dice. They're loaded for seven.

***

Woody Allen Addresses a New Age Convention

To be honest, I don't know why the head
of this group paid me to come. I don't speak
in crystal—I chipped three wineglasses this week.
I don't eat seaweed, yogurt, nine-grain bread.
I don't heal. When sick I hide in bed
and read Kafka or Nietzsche. I don't seek
natural uplift, like fresh air, nor freak
thrills, like out-of-body travel, which I'd dread.
Where Shirley MacLaine wrote *Out on a Limb*,
I directed *Take the Money and Run*.
Where gurus urge to be more like the sun,
I prefer Louie Armstrong, the lights dim.
Last, I'll admit it, I believe in death.
But who wants to volunteer to be out of breath.

***

The Red Skelton Show

Crouched outside the door of their parents' room,
the six-year-old twins wondered: Were Red's bones
dyed in blood? Drawn with scarlet crayons?
Splashed by tomato juice? Dad's funny boom
of a growl made them giggle. The usual gloom
had holes. They wondered: What was going on
with the show that made dad grunt, mother groan,
the noises like laughter out of a tomb.
How could they guess, the two six-year-olds,
what was in store when they furtively cracked
the door, peeked in expecting to behold
mother and dad enjoying some maniac
named Red Skeleton. They found a bedroom dark
but for the dimpled mime escaping a box.

IV

Doctors

When the physician, Dr. Payne,
labeled him incurable, he hissed:
Jerk, rename yourself Hopeless—
I want to speak with your boss.

Next day, upstairs in Dr. Feight's
waiting room, he thumbed the news,
perused an essay that claimed
how an open and loving spirit

could heal even terminal disease,
then asked himself why doctors
too often presumed power, abused
trust, subtly and not-so-subtly

exploited the ill. Was it hubris?
Business? Some sick instinct
to replace mothers and fathers,
please superiors? With Feight,

he would have liked to discuss
the psychology and politics
of medicine, but the head doctor-
administrator led him brusquely

inside. Look, growled Feight
as he shut the door, I know Payne's
a first-class turd, a control freak
who gets jollies when patients squirm,

but the doc's a top diagnostician,
one of the best. I don't know
the story between you and Payne,
don't care to, but I've scanned

the charts—Payne must've wanted
to scare you: the prognosis is off.
A few weeks and you'll be okay;
a month, you'll feel like dancing.

But to be safe, tomorrow morning,
ten o'clock, the walk-in clinic.
Two specialists, Weller and Fein,
will be on call. They can talk.

The Healer

Newly blinded by diabetes,
a young Anchorage doctor
practiced over telephone,
contracting to take calls
from community health aides
in fifteen bush villages.

Greeting the challenge,
he found himself joking
how he'd shut his eyes
when making a diagnosis,
praying to God, kissing
his wife, falling asleep.

Intuition? Faith? Love?
Dream? Whatever, soon
the doctor began to see
shade, shape, the first
faint outline of people.
Miraculously healed

over the next months,
the lucky doctor trumpeted
his dark knowledge as art:
he changed focus, bought tubes
of oils, smeared himself
with smiles, mirrors, light.

The Cure

Impotence is innocence queerly askew,
an embedded wound, no wind.
To cure, begin with a shovel, and enter
this stubborn December earth.

Dig all day, resting frequently, looking about
for signs: a small hole near a mound
of chiseled dirt, a softening chink
of ground, a chipping away of rock.

Grip the shovel hard and resume widening
the circle. Deepen it. As you fling soil
up over, you're reminded of August:
your father's burial. At dusk,

climb out, uncork wine, review the day.
Then shower, eat, listen to jazz, read psychology.
Waking at 3 a.m., you recall a dream: your father,
mining coal in a tunnel, strikes your mother.

Digging in the hole now, thinking
about your father's temper, you're angry.
Weeks pass. Fifteen yards deep, you've carried
down large square stones to construct a wall

with footholds that your father, a practical man,
would have called useful necessities,
like women. He was so cold, so cold
sometimes, your father. A bastard.

And now you understand why your mother
died much earlier. And remembering her now,
your mother, you shovel further
inside, unearthing nuggets with veins.

A find, you believe, and the next day,
in memory of your mother's hopes,
you leave the hole and purchase a bucket,
some rope, wheels, a crank: pulley equipment.

You rig the machinery and descend twelve yards,
fifteen, twenty yards down, foothold
by foothold, handhold by handhold,
lowering yourself past dirt, rock, shadow,

hurrying to the shaft's floor.
In near-darkness, you fill and pull.
The bucket jerks, rope working.
Satisfied, you pick up your shovel

and jab, one thrust disturbing
thousands of worms nested in clumps.
Disregarding the stench, you dig up
maggots and mud, a mushy shovelful

unturning a spring that rushes the bottom.
Carrying the shovel, you climb
the wall, fighting for handholds,
footholds, the way to light.

Pulling yourself over the rim, you inhale
open air. When the gasping subsides,
you grab the crank and wind. At last,
in that pail, your baby boy.

The Contract

Almost two years since you woke slashed
at the right hip, and began vomiting
floods bloodier than birth, disgorging
a twenty-year joining into the toilet.
First, thick torrents of curdled kisses,
unhitched hugs, gassy and crappy whispers.

Then, the slow steady dirt and current
of day-to-day talk, the mud and slag
of magic, your marriage at last thinning
to a milky splatter now and then choked
by gristle and bone, the coughs and gags
of a separation not quite clean.

Now, suffering sporadic nausea, listen
to the queasiness. Eat more simply.
Drink spring water. Cultivate dreams
that surface like air bubbles. Enter one.
Breathe. Celebrate newborn freedom.
You're finally divorced.

The Best Dancers That Night

They boogied for hours
to Chuck Berry, Muddy Waters,
Howling Wolf standards,
her lithe hips shimmying,
her breasts snug in pink
halter top, her smile
like a super-sassy Mona Lisa,
her eyes transfixed on his
as his thick arms and hands
somehow propelled the wheelchair
in loopy maniacal spins
around the nearly full floor.
When the band played a slow one,
she eased astraddle, the gleaming
metal beneath them rocking,
wheels gently rolling.

Houdini's Bondage

Home, they made up
a game: she drove him
with a whip, pierced
his cheeks, snapped him
in cuffs, chained him
spreadeagled to posts.

In turn, he soared
past cloud and moon,
undid wings, donned
collar, saddle, shoes,
and was ridden to Venus,
O magic horse.

For R. S. B., Six Weeks Old, After Surgery

To explain your earthly birth, you
who dangled from the edge
by your toes, we say there must
have been a reason for that near-fatal
appearance, your opening act.
Perhaps it was to toughen you,
and strengthen you, and power you,
and make you especially handsome
and kind. Perhaps it was to fill you
with a particular music and genius,
gifts to inspire and heal. Perhaps,
child, it was to let an old world know
you've arrived late, but loved,
and won't leave, *will not leave,*
until you're through.

Dyxlesia

Yex, like a coded xes dream,
those xynchronicitiex and joyx
that bump friendx together
on a New York xtreet,
or thoxe unespected accidentx
which allow ux to esperience
the world, if only for a moment,
through otherx' eyex
before returning to our own
xtiffening bos of a body—
we're neither blexxed
nor curxed. We are. The bext,
maybe, ix to accept the nest
great inxtant of grace, which,
if we weren't xo buxy xeeking it,
might be greeting ux now.

Depressed Thumb

Because not even penicillin
could ease the infection or pain,
he buried the thumb in wet clay
for an hour, then popped the mottled
flesh with a squeeze, draining
a rich bloody pus that smelled
like the death of his mother.
The emergency room physician
who that night amputated
the half-inch of fingertip
told him that in another day
he very well might have lost
everything to the wrist.

The next weeks, as the mangled
thumb with its jagged black layer
of nail healed between bandagings
and soakings, he pronounced
the word *wound*, and knew
at last his lifelong diminishment
had surfaced. Discarding
the last of the gauze and tape,
peeling a final dented flap
of skin, he unveiled a shorter
stubbier right thumb, a thing
without a print, a reminder
of what had been. And no longer.

The Rewind

My body broke suddenly,
as if I'd overwound
my watch hard past
where the main spring
gave, then wound farther
with the indifference
of a ruined man sticking
the point of a knife
deeper into his gut,
then turning the blade.

I'd wounded myself
that way—carelessly,
coldly. Accident,
I pleaded. Intended,
they said. Sentenced
for a time in solitary,
I thought to listen
to my belly as others
would birds, learned
rumbling bottomless songs.

The Suffering Sestina

Suffering was his first, last, always.
Suffering with a grimace, a grin.
Suffering as if good deed.
Suffering as if dead.
Suffering in order to breathe.
Suffering, he was always suffering.

From him I learned suffering.
God, how we lived. Always
suffering. No one could breathe
in that house. The rare grin.
I was born dead, stayed dead,
died dead. Long years, indeed,

until I left that house. Indeed,
we were not only long-suffering,
we defined suffering. 100% dead,
except to pain, we always
marched with this sick grin
on our faces, afraid to breathe.

So I escaped that house. Breathe,
I said, remembering how. No small deed
relearning inhale, exhale, the grin
and grimace of air. Other lands of suffering,
then, for awhile (for there is always
pain, always suffering). No longer dead,

I crawled past the gray dead
light nearby. I breathed
through that foggy darkness. Always
some new small pain, some slight, some misdeed
to suffer. Even more suffering,
though now I'd grin

through it more often than not. Grin,
I'd whisper. Grin. Through the dead
dark gray, the lighter gray, the suffering,
the brown and yellow pains. I'd breathe
gray, then brown, then yellow. Indeed,
this the way to blue, to green, the always

colorful bruisings. Grin and breathe,
I'd remind myself. Or be dead indeed.
Happy almost always now in the suffering.

Jazz Theory

for Richard Polishuk

Excuse the twelve bad years in pursuit
of perfect pitch, timber, phrasing,
breath. Next, leave the records
and tapes behind, and begin sabbatical,
making your new teacher the hands,
your new instrument the body.
Practicing massage, now listening
to people talk about pain, you find
your thumbs pulsing with tenderness,
your pinkies with strength,
and are struck by what that training
in saxophone lacked: full-blown heart.

The next months, working at the table,
hearing stories, feeling your own
tendons release as you press
and release others, your belief
is like a born-again's. Never
will you allow yourself to be
as you were: self-absorbed, moody,
cynical, asleep, a talented nightmare
of a man. An accomplished bodyworker
of deep compassion, you can return
to your horn, seal it with lips, blow
the music of a wholly content man.

The Massage

On pumpkin-colored walls: framed certificates,
straw hats, bamboo flutes, tambourines,
a cinnamon-red gourd. Lying chest-down
on the table, smelling coconut, he goes
slowly limp as back and buttocks muscles
gets thumbed and squeezed. Surface problems:
a safe but numbing job, a loving wife
he doesn't love, a future promising
nothing. Deeper, a flinch as heels dig
into hamstrings, palms rub knees, fingers
touch bone. Lower: sore calves, an ankle bruise,
cold feet. A shudder as hands probe tendons,
knead soles, pinch and pull toes. A crack
as he's turned over. On his back now,
a softening lump, half middle-aged dreamer
unsure of his way, half homing pigeon
set for flight. Perched atop the gourd, bird
watches man on the table have his scalp
scratched, ears roughed, cheeks smoothed. A coo.
Then, flapping wings shake the shell. Everywhere
maracas, tambourines, flutes, peasants singing
an old island song—*Sleep is for youth,*
In dreams grow old, Love's heavenly truth
flies into the air, Fly out the door,
The breeze is with you, Fly out the door.

In Training

Most evenings, she practices martial arts,
the slow process a physical cleansing
after speedy freeway days. A tensing
and an untensing. Sometimes, as she starts
a kick, she's in the dirt bikes and go-carts
of junior high. Or flashed forward, dancing
a dance she's not supposed to know. Sensing
the future, she remembers to breathe. Hearts
are like hands, she thinks, as she makes fists,
then releases, clasps thin fingers as if
in prayer. She almost feels her right hand insist
a man awaits—this man dreams her—as her left
demands she continue. All night, she fists
and unfists, fists and unfists, fists and unfists...

Wart Stories

I

The wart on the thumb,
treated with acid,
remained spiny, proud
as a cactus.

II

To deaden pain,
a podiatrist
froze the plantar wart—
and the surrounding nerves.

III

Tortured by warts
on chin and nose, the girl
sliced. A week later
new clusters appeared.

IV

The neighborhood
wart healer talked
lovingly to his,
as if they were pups.

V

I cured mine
by signing on
as that wise man's
apprentice.

Treble Choir Was Her World

Inside her throat, light
shined so bright, it grew
into a bird. She named that bird
Voice. It sang and sang.
Dance teachers tried to quash it
with point shoes. Art teachers
tried to tar its white feathers
with paints. Schoolteachers
tried to talk it to death.
Voice only knew to fly
out of her mouth
and soar for the flock.

Stutterer

Valedictorian despite the near-crippling
speech impediment that aroused snickers
from insensitive classmates, the stutterer
took the microphone at graduation, smiling
like a master conjurer about to produce
a rabbit, and, true enough, next moment
a beautiful girl no one had seen before
wheeled herself to the podium, shook
the stutterer's hand, then spoke
to the assemblage about the trampoline
accident that fractured her spine,
the difficult weeks of pain and denial,
the long grieving, the slow recovery,
the final time she felt like killing
herself, the stigmas and challenges
of disability, the compassionate
hard-won love she held for humanity
because all were fellow sufferers,
and concluded by rising from her chair,
embracing the stutterer fiercely
before flapping once, like a raven,
and disappearing into his breast.

A Happier Doctor

for Julia

Yet another practice to begin. Magic
maybe, doctor as juggler, a dozen
roles cascading: mother and daughter;
wife, midwife, analyst; linguist
and listener; dancer, driver, chef;
healer and boss. Ah, the losses
you can now accept, the lives unlived:
local activist, global wanderer, Olympic
gymnast, grant-mad research guru, hermit
glassblower, book critic for *The Times*.
Some late afternoon in that blessed space
between patients, you'll have to place
the stethoscope to your own heart,
replay that path from happy to happier,
make the first move toward happiest.

The Unwinding

Slowly, like a snake uncoiling
from a nap in the sun,
aching muscles and joints lengthen
and stretch with a snap

and spasm, then slip into place
an invincible inch stronger
and looser each repetition.
As the last of the pain

disappears in the deafening
vacuum of a silent bang,
nature celebrates its work:
this dry paper skin left behind.

www.ingramcontent.com/pod-product-compliance
Lightning Source LLC
Chambersburg PA
CBHW051849040426

42447CB00006B/769